How to Get Your *Choral Composition* Published

The Composer as Artist
The Composer as Business Person

Barbara Harlow

SANTA BARBARA MUSIC PUBLISHING

PUBLISHED BY
SANTA BARBARA MUSIC PUBLISHING
P.O. Box 41003
Santa Barbara, California 93109

First Printing, July 1995
10 9 8 7 6 5 4 3 2 1

Library of Congress Catalog Card Number: 95-092355

Harlow, Barbara.
    How to Get Your Choral Composition Published

ISBN 0–9648071–0–6

To the aspiring composer:

May knowledge of the process
join with inspiration
to bring success
to your endeavors.

CONTENTS

THE COMPOSER AS ARTIST

Chapter four
PITFALLS TO AVOID–
GUIDELINES TO FOLLOW

Vocal techniques, a primary consideration
The vocal line
The meter and the word accent
Words: their sound and their meaning
The key signature
Divisi
Your style as a composer
The worst pitfall: Lack of training

THE COMPOSER AS
BUSINESS PERSON

Chapter five
THE SUBMISSION

Is your piece worthy of a submission?
Choose a publisher
When to call a publisher
The cover letter, the SASE, the package
Copyright concerns
The score you submit

Chapter six
INTERACTING WITH A PUBLISHER

The reject notice
The contract
Working with an editor
Proofing your piece
The piece that goes "out of print"

FOREWORD

This is a most welcome book for the aspiring choral composer. Drawing upon her experiences as music publisher, conductor, composer and teacher, Barbara Harlow offers very practical approaches and useful information concerning both the creative process involved in choral composition and guidelines to the process of publication.

Part One discusses important areas of special concern for the choral composer, including choice of text, understanding the choral medium, types of settings, accompaniments and vocal techniques. Following each chapter are checklists for the composer to insure that these topics are carefully considered.

Part Two deals with the composer as a business person and gives invaluable advice on how one goes about the publication process, including the selection of a possible publisher, preparing the manuscript, issues of copyright, contract and proofreading, and related business issues. These techniques and procedures, which always must be carefully thought out and planned, have proven highly successful in publishing numerous works by students enrolled in my own composition and arranging classes at the University of Southern California.

Barbara Harlow's book is a fine introduction to many of the issues related to choral composition and the process of publication which will greatly assist the inexperienced choral composer who, like I, is irresistibly drawn to that most wonderful and fulfilling art—setting poetry to music.

Morten Lauridsen

Professor and Chair of Composition
University of Southern California School of Music
Composer-in-Residence, Los Angeles Master Chorale

REFLECTIONS
AND
ACKNOWLEDGMENTS

The process of getting a choral composition published begins with the birth of an idea for an artistic creation. Hence, the "Composer as Artist" takes the lead in this book. The art of composing is undeniably a lifelong study. The discussion of artistic considerations in this book is intended to open the door a tiny crack to challenge the aspiring composer to want to learn more. To facilitate this learning, it is the author's hope that the recommended book list of future editions of this book can grow to include contemporary publications on the art and craft of choral composition.

The experience of writing this book was enriched by conversations with successful composers. In each case, the composer enthusiastically embraced the book's mission and offered special insights and wisdom. Several composers came up with "gems" that have been woven into the fabric of the book. These acknowledged quotes offer a legacy of inspiration for today's and tomorrow's choral composers. Thank you to each of these special, caring composers: Emma Lou Diemer, Morten Lauridsen, Kirke Mechem, Ben Allaway, David Conte, James McCray, and Libby Larsen

This acknowledgment would not be complete without a big thank you to my family and friends who searched for errant commas and unclear verbiage, and who gave support much as an audience would a performer.

And, to David Harlow, youngest of the three beloved Harlow sons, thank you for the "Idea." As a mainstay in the Santa Barbara Music Publishing operation, he saw a need and suggested, "Write a book that tells how to get a choral piece published."

Barbara Harlow
June 21, 1995

PART ONE

THE
COMPOSER AS
ARTIST

PREPARE TO COMPOSE

You have a goal, a dream, and you are excited about it: you want to compose a piece for a choir to sing and you hope to get the piece published.

There are many creative decisions you face before you begin to compose this piece. What kind of choir will sing your piece? Do you want to arrange a piece or write an original composition? If you choose to compose an original piece, what will you use for a text? Will you use accompaniment and if so, what kind? What style will you choose, contemporary, avant-garde, traditional, folk? How long do you want the piece to be? What key will you use? What meter?

You must decide what "tools" you will use before you begin, just as a painter does before beginning to apply paint to a canvas. Set limitations within which you can create. Igor Stravinsky says of this process:

> My freedom consists in my moving about within the narrow frame that I have assigned myself. My freedom will be so much the greater and meaningful the more narrowly I limit my field of action. [1]

Stravinsky further supports his view by quoting the famous artist Leonardo da Vinci:

> Strength is born of constraint and dies in freedom. [2]

With this in mind, let us begin.

2

TEXT—POETRY
THE WORDS OF A COMPOSITION

Choose a Text

Among the creative decisions you face before taking up the "pen" to compose, the most important is the choice of text. It is the text that will inspire the music, set the mood, and help define what you will do.

Perhaps the text you choose is only one word, *Alleluia,* or a simple phrase, *Sing to God,* or nonsense syllables such as *Fa la la.* Or perhaps it is a sentence taken from a newspaper, or a composite of several poems, or one complete poem. The possibilities are innumerable. When choosing a text, find one you love, one that moves you, one in which you hear music.

Start your search for a text with a particular type of choir in mind. The lyric that appeals to a high school girls' choir may be entirely inappropriate for a children's chorus. Consider the narrowness of your decision. Will children be able to sing this piece only on Easter Sunday? Will it only be appropriate at a funeral or a wedding? Was the text created to honor a special person on a special occasion? Specific usage requirements such as these will limit the possibility of the piece getting performed and therefore published.

Give yourself an advantage by choosing a text that is well-known. Such a text can give the beginning composer an edge when trying to get published. Your own name will not carry recognition with it. The familiar title of your piece will. Publishers are in business to sell music. Anything that can help do this will bring your piece closer to being published.

Explore poetry anthologies for possible texts. If you find a poet you like, go to the poet's collected works for additional possibilities. As the cook collects recipes and the comedian, funny stories, the choral composer collects poetry.

Be cautious about the length of the text you choose. A page-long text may easily turn out to be a ten-minute choral work. We will later learn of the difficulties in getting such a work published. Most important, the short text offers the best direct communication with an audience. Handel was expert at this. In his *Messiah*, the chorus titled *Glory to God* is forty-nine measures long. The complete text:

> Glory to God in the highest,
> and peace on earth, good will towards men.

Kirke Mechem, prolific San Francisco-based choral/opera composer, counsels the composer "to not choose a text with long 'high-falutin' words." He suggests, "Simple, natural language (as found in the King James version of the Bible and in the works of the great lyric poets) makes for better vocal music." These texts often possess the advantage of being well-known. Again, this can be a plus when you are trying to get a piece published.

Are you a fine poet? If so, you may wish to write your own text. Do so knowing that you will be asking a publisher to invest not only in your music, but your poetry. If you are not an expert, it is best to leave that part to a "real" poet. You need to start from strength—a strong text, not a weak one.

A college teacher tells of the student who proudly presented his choral piece, written with no text. The student's plan: to next create a text for the four part composition he had written. The student succeeded, but only after rewriting the music to fit the text he created. It is easier to buy clothes to fit than to try to change your size to fit the clothes you buy! This student will start with a text next time.

Get clearance to use the text

If the poem you have chosen is by a living poet, or one who has died within the last fifty years, even if the poet is (or if deceased, was) a special friend, get written permission to set the poem to music *and* to get it published. This permission must come directly from the owner of the copyright. If the poem is not published, the poet owns the copyright. If the poem appears in a book, the copyright is owned by the publisher of the book. In the latter case, write to the publisher who will in turn contact the poet or the executor of the poet's estate, the person now receiving the royalties on the sales of the poem. The publisher will describe the project and ask permission for you to use the poem, then inform you when that permission has been granted or denied. This can take some time, so plan ahead, and be patient and persistent. If you do not hear from the publisher within a month or so, write again, or call.

Poets and their publishers are usually happy to have their poems set to music and sometimes will grant permission with no strings attached. Occasionally, if the poem has great commercial popularity, permission may not be granted. Or, along with permission to use the poem, you may be asked to sign a contract whereby you agree to share your royalty profits with the holder of the copyright. Or, as is becoming the custom today, the poet/publisher may agree to a flat fee. It is important to know all this up front. Sad is the composer with piece in hand who cannot gain permission to have it published or even sung.

Explore the public domain

A safe text to choose is one in the public domain. A poem enters the public domain fifty years after the death of the poet. The copyright then becomes null and void and the poem can be used by anyone for any purpose with no permission required.

The poems of Walt Whitman, John Greenleaf Whittier, Robert Browning, Samuel Taylor Coleridge, Christina Rossetti, and Robert Louis Stevenson are all in the public domain and are favorites of composers.

A good source for public domain texts is music you already know, texts that were never protected by copyright. There are hundreds of settings of the *Ave Maria* text. And of *Jubilate Deo, Cantate Domino,* and *Ave Verum Corpus.* The bible is a good source of texts in English, particularly the Book of Psalms. Many of these texts have the advantage of being familiar and loved.

Folksongs of unknown origin fall within the public domain. Instead of a poet's name on the music, the word 'traditional' will appear. A text from a folksong can be set to a different melody giving it a new image. This, however, is not recommended if the folksong is a favorite. People have a strong attachment to a melody such as *Amazing Grace.* Few dare tread on such tradition.

Although the writer of a folksong text is unknown, the text may be under copyright to someone as a result of publication and popularization of the song. Search for the original version in an archive collection at a college. To be on the safe side, create your own version by changing a word or two. (Often there are many versions of a folksong text.) State that your text is derived from the original and give the source as part of the documentation of the piece.

You may choose to use a public domain poem that has previously been set to music. If the piece is an established part of the literature, be sure what you envision for your treatment of the text is original and new. The appearance of the music on the page and therefore the sound of the piece should be entirely different from the one already achieving acclaim. If the original was a cappella, use piano. If it was for mixed voices, set it for women. Use a different meter, a different key, a different style, a totally new approach. There is nothing worse than an imitation of a work of art.

The foreign language text

As our country's population becomes more multi-cultural, so does the music we perform. Today's directors are often willing to work with texts in a wide variety of foreign languages. If you choose a text in a language other than English, use that language as the primary text for your piece. Then create an alternate English version being careful to maintain the original meaning. The English text will appear below the original text in the score. Publishers will be more interested in the foreign language piece if a fine English version is included. Get a translation of the foreign text, word by word. (You will need this to set the text to music.) And be prepared to provide a guide to pronunciation. Your publisher should want to include both of these in the publication. You should insist upon it.

The poem and the poet

Learn about the poem and the poet. Increase your inspiration by doing some research. If the poem has deep significance—it was written upon the death of the poet's husband, or the birth of a daughter, or the launching of a space rocket, or the ending of a war, or the dawning of spring after a horrible winter —you must be informed. Find out something of the poet's life. Did he/she live in the ghetto of a big city, or the mountains of Colorado? The poet is a creator just like you and you are now about to go to work "with" him or her. Respect this person by learning all you can about him/her. Request that this information be included with the publication so the people who sing your piece can likewise be informed, enlightened, and hopefully inspired, as were you!

Text:
Checklist for the composer

- Type of choir targeted for the piece
  (i.e., SA children, SATB adult)

- Recommended usage of piece
  (i.e., sacred-church, secular-school, secular-adult community)

- Title of poem

- Name of poet

- Name of translator

- Source of poem
  (book, magazine, tombstone, sign, etc.)

- Written clearance to use text

- Public domain
  (composer deceased for fifty or more years)

- Name of copyright holder

- About the poet
  - Birthplace
  - Dates of life
  - Biographical data
  - Circumstances under which poem was written,
    special significance

- Original language of the poem
  - Word by word translation on file
  - Pronunciation guide on file
  - English version written maintaining meaning of original

CREATIVE DECISIONS

Having chosen a text, you are now ready to make other decisions that will help direct you as you compose your piece.

The type of choir

From the outset, you should have had a type of choir in mind. Learn all you can about that kind of choir before starting to compose. Ask appropriate choral directors for some pointers. Church choir directors may tell you they prefer pieces that have accompaniments, pieces that can be learned quickly. High school choral directors may tell you their men's groups are incapable of singing four-part arrangements, or that they are not allowed to use music that has the word "God" or "Lord" in the text. Children's choir directors may implore you to keep the range in the head voice—on the treble staff, not below it. Junior high directors may caution you about the tenor range, and about the difficulty level of the music. If you do not have directors to consult, go to a music store that specializes in choral music and ask to see best-selling pieces in the area of your choice. Buy single copies and analyze them in terms of difficulty, range, and style. Start your composing with limitations in mind that address the needs of a type of choir.

The genre of the composition

Define the text you have chosen in terms of a genre of composition: the motet, the madrigal, the ballad, the part-song, the hymn, the carol, the anthem, or the spiritual.

With the popularization of chant, the creative door is open for today's composers to use chants in motet settings. For choral musicians, the love of such music is nothing new. Roger Wagner began thousands of concerts conducting his Chorale in the motet *Ave Maria,* by sixteenth century composer Tomás de Vittoria. The audience knew it was in for an exquisite performance after the six-note chant that introduces this motet. You are free to use this genre in many ways. A motet is not limited to the thematic use of a plainsong chant. It is the polyphonic musical style and the sacred text that will classify the piece as a motet. Bach, Brahms, and Bruckner all created masterpieces in this genre.

The madrigal proliferated in the sixteenth century along-side the motet. If you have chosen a light-hearted text that speaks of love, or of nature as a metaphor for love, the intimate madrigal style may be ideal. Notice the word intimate. A madrigal is meant to be sung by a small group. In the sixteenth century, the practice often was to sing madrigals after dinner while still seated at the table, usually one singer on a part. The madrigal is a favorite genre of contemporary composers. Norman Dello Joio, Emma Lou Diemer, Morten Lauridsen, Stephen Paulus, James McCray, Halsey Stevens, Jean Berger, and Daniel Pinkham are some of the many contemporary composers who have written madrigals.

A ballad is a story-telling narrative. The story often deals with love. Two famous ballads from the folk repertoire have love as their themes: *Barbra Allen* and *Frankie and Johnny*. Contemporary composer Halsey Stevens chose the story of a rugged pioneer for his *Ballad of William Sycamore*. The ballad affords great freedom of musical style and presents the opportunity to use a wide variety of texts.

In the broadest sense, "song" is often the label applied to all sung music. As a specific genre, a song tells a story in the first person. "Part-song" is the label given to four-part homophonic compositions with the melody in the top voice. The definition of "song" may or may not be included in this designation. In Samuel Barber's part-song, *The Coolin*, the first person text by James Stevens opens: "Come with me under my coat..." As with the ballad, there is great creative freedom in choosing to write a part-song. You will create your own limitations based on the text and the type of choir you envision.

We think of the hymn as being part of a hymnal. The genre can reach far beyond the hymnal in its style. It is the sacred text and often the title that defines the piece as a hymn. Richard Felciano's concert piece *Hymn of the Universe* is avant-garde in style and uses a text that is a sophisticated poem by Teilhard de Chardin. Benjamin Britten's *Hymn to Saint Cecilia* is an ode to the patron saint of music, the text by W. H. Auden. The limitations of the hymn are only bounded by the composer's imagination.

The carol is a short piece written to a text appropriate for Christmas (or sometimes Easter or a season of the year.) A carol may be secular or sacred. The Alfred Burt *Carols* are among the few to have worked their way into the standard Christmas repertoire. It is a great challenge for a composer to create an original Christmas carol that "catches on" when so many standard ones are available to the conductor. Christmas is a time when people like to be surrounded by people *and* music they love. A college director performed a setting of the *Silent Night* text that used a different melody. The minister of the church where the concert was held expressed great displeasure that he didn't get to hear the real *Silent Night.* (The next year the director and choir pleased the minister with a beautiful setting of the traditional carol.) Composers seeking publication usually have the greatest success arranging existing carols, not in composing new ones.

The anthem traditionally features a sacred text and is meant to be performed in a church setting. Stravinsky wrote his *Anthem,* subtitled *The Dove Descending Breaks the Air,* the text by T.S. Elliot, using a serial tone row. He managed to create a sound that seems to have emerged from the Renaissance. This piece was written at the invitation of the Cambridge University Press to be included in an English hymnal. Note! Stravinsky had a publisher before he began. Unless you have a publisher seeking you out, it is best to choose a style that is accessible to the average church choir.

The spiritual is a staple of choral literature. It features a sacred text, often one in the public domain. Traditionally, a spiritual is a rhythmic and soulful expression of the text. With performance opportunities in both churches and concert halls, the fine spiritual often becomes a best seller. Hence it is a favorite of publishers.

Perhaps none of these describe your ideas for your composition. Invent your own genre. It is important that you make a plan for yourself before you begin, that you set stylistic limitations within which you can work.

The arrangement

Beginners often succeed in getting a piece published by choosing to arrange a song they know: a folksong, a Christmas carol, a hymn tune, or a song by a famous composer. In order to avoid copyright entanglement, it is best to make your choice from music in the public domain. As with poetry, fifty years after the death of the composer, the music enters the free area of the public domain and arrangers can do as they will with it. As with text in the public domain, a particular version of a folksong may be under copyright to an arranger. Do not work from a popular version. Go to the original source and create your own version. And beware, some composers write in the folk idiom. The piece you think is a folksong may not be! Research the origin of the piece carefully before you begin. Otherwise, you might find yourself in court with a legal suit against you.

If you want to arrange a piece that is not in the public domain, by law you must get permission from the copyright holder before you begin. Permission to arrange popular music for publication can be hard to come by. One young composer arranged twenty-five pieces for his school jazz choir without getting prior permission. After he left the position, he decided to take time to try to get the arrangements published. With the assistance of ASCAP and BMI (more about them later), he located the names of the publishers. Sadly, he found he could not get permission to seek publication of *any* of the pieces. In each case the pieces were "standards." The publishers owning the copyrights had arrangements of the pieces already in print. They were not interested in inviting competition for these arrangements.

Should you get permission to arrange a piece and to seek its publication, the holder of the original copyright may want a large percentage of the money you receive from the sales of the piece. The exception: the copyright owner is a publishing house interested in publishing your arrangement. In this case you should receive the standard royalty due an arranger.

Before embarking on arranging any piece, check *Music in Print,* a reference book often available at a university music library (see appendix) to find out what arrangements of the title are available. Or check with your choral music retail expert. Some stores now have the catalogs of all publishers available on a computer database and are able to search for any title. Get copies of the pieces and look them over to determine if your idea is sufficiently original to warrant a new arrangement. And for future reference, make note of the publishers who have published your title. It is unlikely they will be interested in a second arrangement of a title unless it is dramatically different from the one they currently market.

Whatever the song you choose to arrange, your challenge will be to maintain the flavor of the original while adding some new dimension of interest. As arranger, you will ride on the coat-tails of the reputation of the original piece. If a genre is chosen that is currently popular, the opportunities for publication increase. Arrangements of American black spirituals were once much sought after. Today, folksongs from all other countries are a primary interest to choral directors and hence to publishers. As interest changes with time, the savvy arranger chooses to arrange accordingly.

The piece with piano accompaniment

A fine piano accompaniment adds texture, color and style to the piece. It has a function. It is not just a crutch for the singers. On its most demeaning though no less important level, it serves to give the singers their pitches for entrances. At its most creative level, it adds a dimension to a piece that could not be achieved otherwise.

Introductions and interludes should be thought of as moments when the piano can be the star. With the intro-duction, the piano sets the mood of the piece. Sometimes it presents thematic material to be used later on in the voice parts. Composers often have fun with their keyboard parts, assigning them roles in a drama. Perhaps the keyboard is the ocean in a piece about the sea, or a dog in a piece about cats. Study the piano parts of the art songs of Schubert. In his *Die Forelle, (The Trout),* the piano takes the part of a babbling brook. It is a major participant in the drama.

If you are an accomplished pianist, you may err on the side of complexity. If you are an unskilled pianist, your accompaniment may lack sophistication. Protect yourself from either situation by seeking second opinions from choir accompanists. Most can quickly tell you if the accompaniment is playable, suitable, and good.

The piece with organ accompaniment

We think of the organ, and we think of sacred music. We all know, organs are found in churches. They are rarely found in concert halls or school auditoriums. If you choose to use an organ for your accompaniment, it is best that the piece be sacred if publication is what you seek. Secular pieces with organ are rare in today's market.

As with the piano, the organ part should add something special to the piece and set the mood. A church choir may be limited in what it can perform after one Wednesday evening rehearsal. The organ part can add great flare to the easy choral anthem and contribute to the overall quality of the piece. Introductions and interludes can be extended to lessen the demands on the choir. As with the piano accompaniment, these parts should not be thought of as filler. They offer a time when the instrument is the star. Make them special.

A pianist writing for organ should consult an organist regarding registrations and pedal usage. The score destined for submission to a publisher must include proper information for the playing of the instrument, documented in the traditional manner.

Use of other instruments

Many instruments are available to the composer, either alone, or in combinations. Some carry a stereotype with them. The harmonica conjures up cowboys; the trumpet, festive fanfare; the flute, an obbligato above the singers; the bass or vibraphone, a jazz rendition; finger cymbals, an early music piece; the guitar, a folk or Spanish piece; conga drums, an African song. Consider these stereotypes and follow them, *or* reject them. Creative is the composer who uses an instrument in a fresh, new way.

The violin, cello, clarinet, and oboe each can add an interesting dimension to a choral composition. Use the instrument alone, or choose two for a duet. The piano or organ may or may not be part of this accompaniment.

As you choose your instrumentation, consider the availability of players. If you decide on three oboes, you are in trouble. Lucky is the choir director who can come by one good oboe player. Some instruments can be played by choir members. This is always a safe route. Percussion players are in abundance. Good trumpeters are not. Many a fine choral piece has been destroyed by a trumpeter on a bad day. If you write for a large instrument such as a harp, know that the piece will not likely go on tour. Composers often write the harp part so it may be played on the piano if a harp is not available. Finding a good harpist may be difficult. Moving the harp from place to place can be impossible. One composer tells of writing a commissioned composition that included a part for harmonica. The choral director who commissioned the piece could not find a harmonica player who was able to read music. The composer finally agreed to the part being played on a synthesizer. This same composer earlier had similar trouble with a mandolin part—it ultimately got played by a guitarist. If you choose esoteric instruments, plan on being flexible regarding substitution.

Today, synthesizers are abundant and any keyboard player can play one given a little instruction on operation. A synthesizer is capable of creating a myriad of sounds. Add spice to your composition with a fun sound, or one that is mysterious that only a synthesizer can create.

The a cappella piece

The voice is a beautiful instrument on its own. Some of the most precious choral music is un-accompanied. Study the a cappella choral music of Benjamin Britten, Johannes Brahms, Felix Mendelssohn, Igor Stravinsky, and Samuel Barber. You will find these masterpieces are in four parts, they rarely use divisi, and they achieve marvelous color and style.

Study the motets of the Renaissance for melodic independence of parts, and perfection of voice leading. For sophisticated harmonic development, the *Chorales* of Johann Sebastian Bach still stand as the all-time best examples.

A cappella music often is more difficult to perform than music with accompaniment. The singers must rely only on themselves for tonal, harmonic, and rhythmic security. The composer's challenge is to write a piece at once interesting and singable.

Kirke Mechem advises inexperienced composers, "If you want to get published, do not submit a twelve-part atonal a cappella piece no matter how wonderful you think it is." Often young composers fresh out of college look to their college accomplishments for future success. The difficult piece that impressed the college professor and the college choir is unlikely to impress the publisher. (If your name is Aaron Copland, the publisher will be anxious to get your twelve-part atonal a cappella piece.) Mr. Mechem further said, "After I had achieved some success, the same publisher who earlier had refused a piece, now agreed to publish it." Name recognition takes time to establish. While waiting for that to happen, keep your music accessible to many choirs. Pay your dues, as the saying goes. This will reap you profit and future rewards.

The soloist
as part of the choral composition

The choral piece that features a soloist seldom becomes a big seller. The reason: many choirs do not have the soloist needed to perform the piece. Hiring an instrumentalist to be a part of a concert is common-place. Hiring a soloist to perform a short piece with a choir is less common. If you choose to write a solo voice part, make the part accessible. The ranges and the demands must not be extreme. And, it should be the kind of piece that could not be written any other way. Narrative spirituals sometimes utilize a soloist. One immediately thinks of *Amen* by Jester Hairston, an all-time favorite in this category.

The incidental solo is much more common. The piece begins with a solo and the choir enters later. This solo is often labeled "optional"—an entire section may sing it if a soloist is unavailable. This is the safest kind of solo to write as it carries no limitations with it.

A composer may choose to insert a solo to highlight a special part of the text, one which needs a soloist to impart the message. Amateur writers often fail in this regard. If the supporting parts are not voiced carefully, the solo will not stand out. It is difficult to set up a solo that suddenly appears without it seeming detached from the rest of the piece. The solo that makes a final statement in a piece followed by a short choral conclusion is the most effective of this type. Performance alone can prove the success of the incidental solo.

The set of pieces vs. the extended work

If you wish to compose an extended work, your possibilities for publication decrease greatly. It is better to create a set of short pieces. Publishers are much more willing to invest in a set of three short pieces that can be published separately than in one long one. They know one piece in the set may become a big seller, one may be weak, and only a few people will perform the entire set as a group. Like investing in a mutual fund, this type of investing diversifies the publishers' interests and protects them from losses. If you look at the output of most publishing houses, you will find very few large works being published in a year's time. Yet a publishing house may release fifty or more shorter pieces during this same year. Because of the prohibitive cost of production and promotion, some publishers accept no extended works as a matter of policy .

If you choose to write a set of pieces, they should be related by subject matter. The text might be several poems, or one extended poem divided into sections. Famous examples are Benjamin Britten's *Five Flower Songs*, Samuel Barber's *Reincarnations.*, and Morten Lauridsen's three choral cycles, *Mid-Winter Songs*, *Madrigali*, and *Les Chansons des Roses*. The set of pieces should be of similar difficulty so that one choir would be able to perform them all. They should use various keys that relate like movements of a symphony. Their meters should fit the individual texts and be different for each piece. Like rooms of a house, each piece should be unique while working together as an architectural entity.

Creative decisions:
Checklist for the composer

- Title of piece
- Type of choir
- Genre of piece
- Accompaniment
- A cappella
- Use of soloist

PITFALLS TO AVOID
GUIDELINES TO FOLLOW

Emma Lou Diemer, versatile Santa Barbara composer, advises, "Write something that is unique and fresh within the boundaries of what is practical and accessible."

The composer who is a creative artist will find a way to be unique and fresh. If the composer is also skilled at the craft of writing for a choir, great may be the results. If that craft is not evident, a publisher will not be interested in the music no matter how clever it may be.

Vocal techniques, a primary consideration

If you were to compose à solo piece for guitar, you would need to know a great deal about playing that instrument before you could begin. The voice, too, is an instrument. It poses limitations of which you must be aware.

The most obvious limitation is range. Choose the correct range for the choir targeted to perform your composition. You will find suggested ranges in the appendix of this book. Beginning composers often err with one single note—i.e., the low C for the basses at the end of the composition. The composer says, "It is only one note." Yes. And if that final chord is important, and it had better be, the low C must sound. Basses that can sing low C's are extremely rare. A publisher may immediately eliminate the piece knowing that directors will not choose it because of this one note. The same can be said for high B's and C's for tenors and sopranos, and low E's for altos. These represent the extremes of adult vocal ranges. Avoid them because they are not accessible, or use them knowing that only the most vocally endowed choirs will be able to perform the piece.

A secondary element of range is tessitura, the average range of the piece. Beethoven is famous for writing the voice parts of his *Missa Solemnis* and *Ninth Symphony* at the very top of the vocal range in a constantly high tessitura. He wanted the singers heard over the orchestra. This produced a beautiful result, but is a singer's nightmare. Whole sections of professional choirs have been known to finish repeated performances of these works with sore throats. Stravinsky came along years later and left the violins, violas, and clarinets out of his *Symphony of Psalms*. His goal: to have the chorus and the orchestra be "equals." This planning resulted in comfortable ranges for the singers, and a stunning balance between orchestra and choir. Your goal as composer should be to create a sensible tessitura for your singers. Both they and their audiences will appreciate your consideration.

Be careful of the vowel choice in relation to pitch. The word "see" on a high soprano pitch is a poor choice. The singer will have to modify the ee vowel toward uh in order to sing it. The meaning of the word will be lost. Rule: closed vowels ay and ee do not work well on high pitches.

Give the singer time to breathe. If rests for breaths are not part of the plan, indicate that the part use staggered breathing, each singer breathing on his/her own. If the breaths are to be catch breaths in the middle of a long phrase, indicate them with a breath comma and know that the line will be broken somewhat at that point.

Vary the dynamics. Continuous double forte singing is hard on the voice. So is continuous pianissimo singing. For expressive singing, dynamic variety is essential.

The Vocal Line

The best test of your choral writing is to sing each part. The first judgment: is the part singable? Awkward leaps signal poor writing. Most vocal writing is conjunct, stepwise, linear. Disjunct writing can be very difficult to sing. Famous melodies can provide great insight into the use of intervals. *The Sound of Music, Maria* from *Westside Story, Joy to the World,* and *Silent Night* are a few you might consider. Look at the choral pieces you love. Analyze their vocal lines in terms of the intervals used.

The second test: is the part interesting? Choral singers love to sing the works of Benjamin Britten because he shares the interesting moments among the parts. All voices are equally challenged. Strive for interesting part writing. Give each voice part a chance to be the star.

Does the writing appear to be pianistically conceived? For special effects, piano-style imitations are fine. The choir imitates the piano sounding a waltz accompaniment, or the piano playing a broken chord. The test is in the singing Are the individual vocal lines thought out carefully, or do they simply fall where the fingers of the piano player landed?   If the latter is the case, the vocal line may be difficult and awkward.

Unison singing presents an opportunity for the entire choir to enjoy the melodic spotlight, and it is beautiful. Put this high on your list of tools for composition. Your only restraints relate to range. Be conservative so the sections of the choir assigned the solo can sing the melody with ease.

James McCray tells his Colorado State University composition students to imagine they are singing in a choir. "Ask yourself," he says, "what kind of a part do you like to sing?"

The meter and the word accent

David Conte, San Francisco Conservatory of Music composer/teacher, suggests that composers memorize any text they are going to set. He says, "Be able to recite the text aloud from memory from beginning to end before you write a note. This will insure that you have internalized the rhythm, meter, tone and shape of the poem in the most organic way."

Say the text of your piece aloud and feel the meter it imparts. Does it sound at home in three, in four, in compound meter? If you find the meter does not fit a regular pattern you may need to use changing meters. Use them only when the words demand, or when they can create an interesting musical design. Changing meters make the conducting and the execution of a piece more difficult, and unless chosen carefully, can destroy a composition. In the following example, a design has been created. The music can dance.

To - mor- row   is   my   danc- ing   day.

34

This same example can be written another way, with no change in meters. Often this is the case. The composer must explore all possibilities and decide which way is easiest for the conductor and the performer.

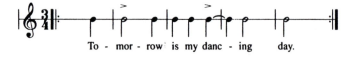

Check the words of your piece. Underline the stressed syllable of each word. Sing the words to hear that the stressed syllables come on the strong beats, *and on the long notes.* If there are exceptions to this, mark those notes with accents as was done in the above example on "*danc-.*"

Occasionally composers use words playfully in a stylized manner ignoring the natural word accent. This is done by design, never by accident. The plan should be clear. In the following example the text is first stated with correct word accents, then with the accents displaced for an interesting variation.

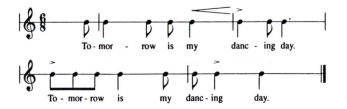

Words: their sound and their meaning

Fine singers will tell you text is everything in a song. All expression, all rhythm, all nuance stems directly from the execution of the text.

Words have sounds which impact music. Some consonants are pitched, others unpitched. Some can be sustained on a pitch, others cannot. Some are aspirates made only of air. A harsh text with many explosive unpitched consonants (K, P, T), and their pitched explosive partners (G, B, D), will conjure up a particular musical style. Conversely, a text with many sustained, pitched consonants such as M, N, NG, L, and V produces another mood. The word "love" contains two sustained, pitched consonants. A common directive of choral directors to singers regarding this word, or its cousin "lovely," is to put ten L's at the beginning of the word—sustain that L. A similar case can be made for M and to a greater degree, MM. The wise choral composer gives these sustained pitches time to happen and uses the short, harsh consonants to create the rhythmic "bones" of the music. Study language for its many possibilities and compose accordingly.

Good poets make a careful choice of words to create drama, a mood, a style. The composer, having chosen a poem, must see inside those words. What can the music do to heighten the drama? Which words should be sustained, which repeated? Which should move fast, which should be accented, which should be staccato?

Libby Larsen, highly respected Minneapolis composer is noted for her clever, often whimsical treatment of text. She says, "The best word setting lets the music flow from the words, allowing the words to set the music." She adds, "Many composers create awkward lines trying to force the words into the music. The words will never let you down if you let them speak, and ultimately, sing for themselves." The three songs of her *And Sparrows Everywhere* are wonderful examples of her text setting skill, of her ability to allow words to "sing." Libby Larsen's choral music is recommended for study.

If a text tells a story, it is important to get to the heart of that story. When David Conte composed his SATB setting of *Psalm 121*, he took into account *who* was singing: the pilgrims as they went up to Jerusalem for the holy feasts. To set this scene of walking up the hillside to worship at the temple, he chose a more flowing, compound meter in an *Andante* tempo. David Conte is known for his sensitive settings of poetry. The wise aspiring composer will collect good examples of text setting and take time to learn what is effective and what is not.

The key signature

Choose a key for your piece but do not be married to it! It may be that after you complete the composition you will discover it will work better in a different key. Examine the ranges and the tessitura with your target choir in mind. If need be, transpose the piece to a new key.

Avoid complicated key signatures. Most keyboard players find six flats or sharps far from practical or accessible. Singers with limited keyboard ability may want to play their parts—difficult keys will make this impossible. If the piece is a cappella and you hear it in the key of G flat, write it in G and indicate that it was originally composed in the lower key. The choir can easily sing it in the original key after all the notes are learned.

Divisi

SATBB, SATTB, SAATB, SSATB. There are obviously many possibilities for dividing the voice parts. Those listed here pose problems for only one section. That section must be larger than the others if the piece is to be balanced. The conductor can sometimes meet this requirement by shifting voices to a different part, asking an alto to cover a second soprano part, or a baritone to sing second tenor.

SSA ATTBB. The complete divisi of parts signals a standard for the group. The choir must be large and capable, preferably made up of good readers, and have good attendance habits so that in rehearsal all parts are consistently covered.

The practical problems with execution of divisi scores cause many directors to avoid such pieces altogether. College directors sometimes spend the first month of the semester finalizing their recruitment. Church choirs often have fluctuating attendance and membership. It is difficult to divide parts when the membership is not established. Divisi music can take more teaching/learning time and it requires more organization on the part of the conductor. Sectional rehearsals now must deal with two parts. Some singers might be doing double duty, singing second soprano part of the time, and first alto other times, depending upon the demands of the score. This adds to the confusion.

Divisi writing sometimes errs in not observing the conventions of writing a good, singable vocal line. The altos jump from two parts to one, they cross awkwardly, there seems to be no plan for what they are asked to do. The composer was thinking chordally, not according to the line. This is difficult music to learn. It will be difficult music for the publisher to sell.

Divisi writing used sparingly is acceptable to most

directors. Typical is the final cadence that fans out to six or eight parts. Revoicing a choir to cover one cadence is worth it if it creates a special ending, a special effect.

Publishers are not eager to accept pieces that feature divisi writing unless it is the work of a well-known master composer. This is a reflection on the state of choral music in our country, not a statement against a style of writing. Again, publishers must publish what they can sell.

Your style as a composer

Good style is always hard to define, yet we can easily sense it when we encounter it. The husband exclaims to his wife, "But didn't you say, brown and blue don't go together?" It is how they are combined that decides if they belong together. So it is with music. Mix your ideas carefully. Be wary of being too creative, using too many ideas in one piece. This is often the sign of a talented beginner. Lacking skill at developing one good idea, the beginner jumps to a new idea. To paraphrase Leonardo da Vinci's creed: too many ideas represent too much freedom and result in a weak creation.

A publisher is quick to sense a piece that has style, and even quicker to sense one that does not.

The worst pitfall: lack of training

Ben Allaway, successful young Iowa composer says, "Composing is an acquired skill. You're not simply born with this ability." Ben suggests that aspiring composers take time to study composition if composing is their goal. Knowledge about musical form, harmonic structure and tension, melodic development, unity, how to add spice to a composition—these are some of the tools you need to enable you to create your own personal style.

All choral composers should have experience not just singing, but singing in a choir. Some fine composers have learned what choirs and singers can and cannot do while serving as accompanist for a choir. In both cases, experience was the teacher. Learn by doing!

As a job, "composer" is at the top of the musical echelon. A composer must know as much as a conductor—he or she is the "instructor" of conductors. The composer must know as much as a performer—he or she is the "instructor" of performers. How do you measure up?

Guidelines and pitfalls:
Checklist for the composer

- Range appropriate for the choir targeted for performance
- Tessitura not excessively high, nor excessively low
- Word (vowel) placement takes pitch into consideration
- Breathing accounted for
- Dynamic variety: list the dynamics used
- The vocal line: sing each line
  - Interesting or boring?
  - Ease of execution
- Use of divisi
  - Which part(s) divide
  - How often?
- Style: list the musical ideas used in the piece

PART TWO

THE COMPOSER
AS
BUSINESS
PERSON

5

THE SUBMISSION

Is your piece worthy of a submission?

The composition you are considering for submission to a publisher should withstand some field trials before going up before the publisher "judge." First, if you are unsure about its worth, get approval from an expert, preferably a composition teacher who specializes in choral music.

Before submitting your piece to a publisher, it should have a performance test, not just by your own beloved choir, but by another impartial choir. Try offering your piece to a choral director who performs music similar to your piece. See what response you get. If you have trouble interesting this choral director (and subsequently, his/her peers) in your composition, it is not likely a publisher will be interested. If a choir performs and loves your piece, and an audience responds well to it, you have a special stamp of approval, one you can share with a publisher.

With the successful test of your piece, you can submit it to a publisher with confidence. The only way to go!

Choose a publisher

Publishing companies are businesses subject to the strengths and frailties of most any business. They have been known to merge, to expand and grow, to stay small and elitist, to specialize, to sell out to another company, to let another company be their distributor, to succeed, and to fail.

Today with computer technology available to all who can afford and deal with it, new publishers, with the help of their composer friends, are continually making their entrance into the market place. Whether the publisher is new or well-established, composers should learn about a publisher before sending a submission.

Some publishers publish all types of music. Others have specialties—school, church, ethnic, pop, "classical," esoteric, or instructional. Some only publish short octavos. Others publish compositions of all lengths, but only by well established composers. It is important to choose a publisher you know seeks the kind of piece you have written, one who will be receptive to you and your submission. Study a publisher's catalog, or take a college choral literature class that examines a wealth of materials, or attend reading sessions, or talk to experienced directors, or examine music at a store with the assistance of a knowledgeable salesperson, or best, do all of the above. If you are active in the mainstream of choral activity you can quickly learn about publishers.

Discover something of a company's marketing style. Call the publisher to request a catalog or a promotional flier of new issues. When you call, take note, does someone answer the phone, or return your call within a reasonable amount of time? Is the material you receive appealing to you?

Look for the publisher's music at a store that specializes in choral music. Is the product, the music, neatly printed and professional in appearance? Ask the choral expert at this store if the publisher supplies music in a timely manner. This person may volunteer additional information depending upon his/her dealings with the publisher.

Check the programs of national American Choral Directors Association conventions, the Choral Journal, the church music magazine you subscribe to—does the company advertise?

Does the publisher belong to professional organizations such as the Retail Print Music Dealers Association, and the Music Publishers Association? Membership suggests the publisher is making an effort to stay abreast of changes and happenings in the industry. You can request member lists from these organizations. The addresses are in the appendix of this book.

Talk to composers who deal with the publishers you are considering. Do they pay royalties in a timely manner? Do they communicate with their client composers, keep them abreast of the business operation much as a company would its stock holders? Do they let a composer know the status of his publications, notify him/her if a piece goes out of print? Do they lose things—manuscripts, copyright documents, the contract? Do they take forever to decide on a submission? Most companies establish good reputations or go out of business. A good reputation should not to be marred by an occasional negative incident. It is the company that has a record of repeated unbusinesslike dealings you must watch out for.

The music business is a tight knit one. A little inquiry and detective work on your part can give you information about how a publisher is perceived in the marketplace today. Your research should result in your discovery of three or more publishers to target for submission of your piece. Plan to make your submission to your first choice. Save the other two should you not receive a contract on your first try.

You may be tempted to submit a piece to more than one publisher. The multiple submission is common among writers for magazines, uncommon among composers. If for some reason you feel you must submit a piece to more than one publisher at a time, be up front about this and include in your cover letter the names of all publishers receiving the submission. If the piece is a fabulous winner, this might result in a quick response from a publisher. You then must immediately let the other publishers know the piece has been accepted and by whom. You run the risk, no matter how you go about multiple submissions, of alienating a publisher too busy to be bothered with such tactics.

If you have several pieces ready for submission you may wonder if you should send them all together to one publisher. Many circumstances come into play. Some will work for you, some against. If you submit five anthems for SATB church choir with organ accompaniment to one publisher, it is unlikely all five will be accepted at once—the pieces are now in competition with each other. An editor may decide he likes none of your pieces. You are now instantly a five-time loser. There is no set rule, but it may be better to let each piece have its turn. Send what you think is best first. The exception to this is the set of pieces—they must be submitted together. The experienced composer who writes mainly on commission, may submit several pieces, each very different from the other. This composer is in a better position to do this than the unknown beginner.

When to call a publisher

You have written a two-minute secular octavo based on an African theme. Should you call and ask a publisher if he would like to see the piece?

If you have done your homework, you know whether or not the publisher publishes two-minute choral pieces such as yours. In order to evaluate your piece, a publisher must see it, not just hear about it. Submit the piece in the mail. Do not call.

Some composers feel compelled to call publishers and ask what kind of pieces they are looking for. The person you talk to might say, "music for school," or "music for church," or simply, "quality music." Or if the person is feeling clever that day he might say, "a piece that will sell one hundred thousand copies!" Again, do your homework on your own to find out what kind of music publishers like as evidenced by their publications. Do not bother a publisher with this kind of phone call.

Save your call for when you have a unique project to offer. Call and ask to speak to the person in charge of editorial decisions. Perhaps you have written a musical for children on a biblical theme, or you are famous for your vocal techniques for young boys and are thinking of making a video, or you are the composer of a Christmas work for choir, orchestra, and five soloists that has been successfully performed by a professional choir.

A person can respond to this type of query and tell you if the company would be interested in a submission of your work.

The cover letter, the SASE, the package

When you prepare the cover letter for your submission you take off your creative rags, and put on your business suit. You have now officially entered into the Business of Music.

Any good business person has letterhead stationery. The exception—if you are a teacher, your school letterhead is fine. For many business reasons, a composer should have a computer. Computers can generate a letterhead and a professional appearing letter. If you are without a computer, have letterhead printed. Or, at the very least, use your typewriter to create a quasi letterhead look. A publisher will sense your effort at professionalism and react favorably.

Address your letter to the editor. If you know the person's name, use it.

In your letter, briefly introduce yourself telling the focus of your current music involvement. We are assuming you are not well-known, a beginner in this business. If you do have other pieces published, you may want to list them along with their publishers. Do not provide a long list of unpublished works. This signals you are a prolific composer and have not had success getting published. The personal introduction may not be necessary for experienced composers. But, even they are wise to include some reference to their current position and to the extent of their publications.

State if the piece was commissioned by, or written for, a particular choir.

List the performances you have had of the piece.

If you have a tape of a performance of which you are proud, include it as an extension of your cover letter. If the tape is poorly performed, do not send it. A bad tape indicates the piece was too difficult for the choir, not an impression you want to send to a publisher.

Some composers like to send synthesizer generated tapes to demonstrate their scores. If the piece is not easily played on the keyboard, this can be helpful—i.e., it is in four parts, plus piano, plus two instruments. However, a tape of a real performance is always preferred.

If you have received praise for the piece, a newspaper review, a special performance, share it.

If a clearance has been received for the poem you are using, include a copy of it with the cover letter.

If the piece requires explanation, provide it. Give the publisher the same background you would provide a conductor. If the piece needs no explanation, give none.

Allow the music to speak for itself.

It is often a good idea to include a printout of the poem along with the submission.

Send along a self-addressed stamped envelope (SASE) if you desire the return of your materials. Publishers receive hundreds of submissions. They cannot be expected to pay return postage.

Kirke Mechem half-jokingly says, "The best submission is accompanied by a list of five choir directors who each want to purchase one hundred copies of the piece!" A publisher will invest money to produce your piece. If you have real customers lined up, don't hesitate to mention them.

Copyright concerns

As "author" of your composition, you own the copyright. You need not register your piece for the copyright to be in force. Today's copyright law, as revised in 1976, does not even require that a copyright notice be printed on a piece in order for that piece to be protected by the law. It is, however, a good idea that you include the copyright sign ©, and the year of copyright on the first page of your music. Reputable publishers have the greatest respect for the copyright law. You can feel safe sending them your piece.

As owner of the copyright, you automatically have

permission to copy your work. Do this judiciously. It is not wise to have numerous photocopies of a piece in circulation if you are pursuing publication.

The score you submit

The score, like the cover letter, should be professional and business-like in appearance. It should bear no resemblance to a hastily created student assignment. It should radiate caring and talent on the part of the creator.

Another reason for getting a computer: computer generated scores look professional in appearance. Some composers are blessed and can write a score as well as any copyist. There is a special beauty in such a score. It immediately reflects experience on the part of the creator. However, most of us breathed a huge sigh of relief when the computer learned to reproduce music, and quickly shelled out the dollars to free ourselves from this difficult task. There are many programs available today, with many more promised. Consult other composers, magazine reviews, online forums, and the publishers of the computer programs themselves to get a perspective on the program that best suits your needs.

Be accurate with your score however you choose to prepare it. Give the music plenty of space. Use correct notation. If in doubt about the conventions of notation, consult published sources to learn what is correct. See the appendix for some recommendations.

Be precise as to the length of crescendos and decrescendos, the choice of dynamic markings, the use of articulation markings, and the use of slurs to indicate multiple notes on one syllable. Keep in mind, the more you indicate to the performer, the closer the performance can be to your intentions. The score that has no performance indications is very weak.

Be precise with the text. If you say "close to N" on a word that receives four beats, name the beat on which you want the N to close. Use the punctuation and capitalization you expect to see in print. Never use all capital letters unless that is what you want for the final result. Consult the dictionary for proper hyphenation of words.

If need be, hire an expert to notate your score. It is not unusual for a composer to employ a copyist. Today, the copyist uses a computer not a pen.

Photocopy the score, and put the copy in a nine by twelve envelope addressed to the editor of the publishing house. Do not fold or staple the pages. Do not weigh down the package with excessive packing materials. Make a record of the date, and keep a copy of the letter and of any documentation you have sent. Send the package by regular mail.

Now, congratulate yourself! If this is your first submission, you have accomplished a singular achievement.

The submission:
Checklist for the composer

- Piece has stood the scrutiny of an expert
- Piece has stood the test of performance
- Publisher chosen publishes the type of piece you are submitting
- Publisher reputation established and personally approved
- Cover letter written in a business-like manner
- SASE included
- Packaging of photocopied score and all materials efficiently done
- Legible, accurate score
- Record kept of date submitted
- Copy of all correspondence on file

6

INTERACTING WITH A PUBLISHER

The reject notice

A large publishing house will have several editors, each one in charge of reviewing a type of music. A small publishing house, and some larger ones that specialize in choral music, might have an owner who serves as editor and reviews every submission. Whatever the case, your piece will be reviewed both as to its merit as a work of art, and as a possible entry into the publisher's catalog.

The reject notice is traditionally an impersonal message sent a composer after the editor has passed judgement on the submitted piece. It might simply read, "We regret we are not interested in publishing your submission." The title(s) will be included in the notice.

Publishers may break with tradition. An editor might choose to call a composer about a piece, perhaps with a change that will make the piece acceptable for publication. Or, the reject notice may consist of a personal letter that provides some insight into the reason the piece was rejected. This letter may contain a directive leading the composer to another publishing

58

house, or it may offer a suggestion to improve the composition.

How nice it would be if a composer could always learn something as to why a piece is rejected. It is not unthinkable for a composer to include a page with the submission offering a publisher the opportunity to provide some insight. Be careful to state your case. You might say, "I am trying to grow as a composer. If this piece is rejected, I would appreciate it if the editor would check the appropriate boxes on this page." Offer the following choices:

- Unsuitable for our catalog
- Does not meet our current needs
- Does not meet our music standards
- Lack of market for this type piece

Editors will respect such an inquiry and should try to see that the page is returned to you with your reject notice.

Some publishers acknowledge the receipt of a submission. If after three months you have heard nothing, inquire if the submission was received. If after six months you have not received a notice of the decision, you may want to request that the piece be withdrawn so you can submit it to another publisher.

The contract

The primary function of a contract is for you, the author, to guarantee the publisher that the work is original and free from copyright encumbrances, and to transfer the ownership of the copyright from you to the publisher. As owner of the copyright, the publisher will be responsible for protecting this interest. Should a copyright infringement occur relative to the piece, it is the publisher's responsibility to resolve the problem. Occasionally this can involve legal action.

If the piece you have written is to have a life beyond that of a choral composition—i.e., it is a pop piece that may later be written as a solo, or in a completely different arrangement such as orchestral—the contract may be written limiting the publisher to ownership of the choral rendition. In this case the composer owns all other rights for use of the piece.

The contract will define the terms of your royalty payment. Ten per cent of the retail price of the piece is the standard royalty. The exception: the arrangement is of a piece whose original composer is living. In this case, the ten percent royalty will be divided equally between composer and arranger. For all royalties, typically payment is set up on an annual basis, usually one or two months after the month of the contract date.

Other items the contract may include: the right of

the publisher to transfer ownership of the copyright upon sale of the company, the right of the publisher to charge a composer for costly errors not corrected in the final proofing of the piece, and the establishment of an amount of payment a composer will receive for mechanical royalties (monies received from recordings and broadcasts of the piece).

If you have serious questions about a contract, consult a lawyer. If you have reservations about some aspect of a contract and want a change made, put this in writing to the publisher. A publisher may or may not choose to honor your request for a change.

Working with an editor

Choral editors are hired by publishers to evaluate the music submitted for publication. They are chosen for the job because they are experts in some area of the choral art and because they have experience composing music.

An editor may make suggestions for changing your piece. If extensive, the contract issuance may depend upon the successful realization of the changes. As composer, you have the final word—if you disagree with the suggestions, you can always withdraw your piece and seek another publisher.

If the suggested alterations are minor, they may be

brought to your attention after you have signed the contract. Again, you have the final word. If you disagree at this point, it should not impact the publication of your piece.

Proofing your piece

Perfection is the goal in all publishing. When it is achieved in the production of a piece of music, everyone is the winner: the composer, the publisher, the conductor, the singer, and the audience. One disastrous story tells of a piece printed with an incorrect metronome marking. This choral part-song by a famous composer was recorded by an equally famous choir. Conductors everywhere emulated this recording. Sadly, the recorded performance was twice as fast as the composer intended—a half note had been indicated instead of a quarter note in the metronome marking.

A composer should plan on taking plenty of time to proof a piece. First, get organized in terms of what needs to be done. Then, be consistent with the procedure any time a proof must be done. Some suggestions:

- Use red pen to mark the error in the score.
- Reference the error in a margin next to the staff where it occurs

Make a checklist for all items you will visually proof:

- Soprano notes
- Alto notes etc.
- Piano right hand notes
- Piano left hand notes
- Dynamics
- Text for each voice part
- All directives (including the M.M. marking)
- Title page—check every word
- Other written documentation—check every word

After the visual proof, play the various parts on the piano. Then, if possible, have someone else proof the piece, if not the music, the textual elements.

Create a separate proof sheet listing the measure number of each error and a description of the error. This eliminates any misunderstanding of markings placed in the score.

Return the proofed music to the publisher keeping a photo-copy of every page you send. You may receive a phone call from the editor with a question. If you have the proof copy on hand for reference, you can respond. Should the proof be lost in the mail or misplaced by the publisher, you will be delighted to have a backup copy.

Proofing does not end when the piece is in print. As

composer, keep a watchful eye and ear. If mistakes are discovered, inform the publisher immediately. A publisher can inform people of the error on a separate errata page until the piece goes into its next printing with a corrected master copy.

The piece that goes "out of print"

There are several reasons a publisher will let a piece go out of print. If a piece is a poor seller from the beginning, the publisher may not reprint it. If, after many years, the sales of the piece decline dramatically, the piece may be removed from the catalog. The sale of a publisher's complete catalog to another company may result in the re-evaluation of the pieces by the new owner. Subsequently, some pieces may go out of print. If the publisher is the type that specializes in trendy music, the music will go out of print when the trend passes.

Whatever the reason, it is the publisher's duty to inform the composer when a piece ceases to be a part of the active catalog. Copies remaining in stock are customarily returned to the composer along with ownership of the copyright.

When this happens, some composers try to remarket the piece. It is best if the composer does something to improve the composition. If it was a fairly new piece that did not sell, there must be a reason. Perhaps it was too difficult, or too limited in its appeal. If it was an older piece, it may need updating. When submitting such a piece, give its publishing history and point out what changes have been made. To not do this is to misrepresent your work.

7

BUSINESS-LIKE ORGANIZATION

Organization is a key component of a successful business operation. Begin your organization system with your first submission and establish a pattern for life.

Organize your scores

Dedicate space in a file cabinet drawer to your original scores. Create a file folder for each piece. When a piece is published, graduate the folder to a special section for published pieces.

In each folder, place the following:

1. The original manuscript
2. A list of submissions and rejections, with dates
3. The signed contract—make a special notation of the date of the contract
4. Copies of the printed piece
5. Correspondence from the publisher regarding the piece
6. A record of royalty payments: the dollar amount received plus the date received

A computer can help you keep records such as those suggested in numbers two and six above. In addition, the original score, if done on computer, can be saved on disk in addition to the paper copy in the file drawer. Many smart business people keep duplicate records: one set at the work place, another off-site. A composer could easily protect himself against the loss of records and music scores due to a disaster such as a fire or theft if computer disks were kept in two places. Too often we hear of creative works lost or destroyed. Proper organization can prevent this occurrence.

Many a reader had a chuckle when the following ad appeared in the church music magazine, *Creator* under the heading, *Searching for an Anthem:* (The name of the oft-published composer, the title of the composition, and the well-known publishing house have been changed.)

> If you have a copy of John Smith's *The Birthday of Freedom*, please call Creator Magazine. It seems the original publisher, C.S.T. PUBLISHING does not, and neither does Mr. Smith.

Publishers do not attempt to keep track of pieces that go out of print. Many creative people get so involved in their work, they do not take time to get organized. The result is in the advertisement.

Your business database

Rolodex files generated by hand are a thing of the past. Database is the operant word today. A computer database can place the important information you need at your fingertips in any format you desire, including Rolodex.

Wouldn't it be wonderful to be able to find the phone number of any person you know, any publishing house and editor with whom you deal, plus the addresses for all of the above instantly?! Input this information into a computer once and organize it however you want—print it out to fit in your pocket, your purse, your briefcase, your file drawer, and for labels for your Rolodex file.

If you have large collections of music, a database can organize the titles, be they compact discs or sheet music or both. Input the title, the composer, the style, the duration, the accompaniment, the media (compact disc or sheet music), and any other information you deem important. Then call up all the pieces in one style, or by one composer, or with flute accompaniment. Or, ask your computer for an alphabetized list of your compact discs and go to a record store with a complete list of your collection in hand.

If a composer does not have time for such computer organization, it may be worthwhile to hire someone to input the data. Time is especially precious for creative people. Better to not waste yours doing something someone else can do. When complete, the computer database is one of the greatest time savers around.

Your business finances

Computer programs are available that can both organize your finances and save you time. The programs are becoming increasingly user-friendly with short learning curves. With a little help and some patience, anyone can simplify the keeping of financial records. A finance program will write checks, balance checkbooks, create reports, furnish tax information, and merge with tax preparation software.

Finance programs keep track of both income and expenditures. Enter any royalty payments received as income. With the entry, attach the publisher name and the piece title, or a code for same. Reports then can be generated for a year telling how much was received from each publisher and for each piece. Or a report can tell you how much any one title has earned over its lifetime.

Expenditures that relate to your composing can be entered as tax deductible items. These expenditures will include your computer and all peripherals that go with it, your home office and its supplies, your musical instruments, the tuning and maintenance of your piano, your fax and phone lines, concert tickets, convention travel, professional dues and subscriptions—anything that is involved in or related to your business of composing. The only catch: to be acceptable as legitimate tax deductible expenses, you must show income as a composer.

When tax time rolls around, use your computer to print out a report of all income received and all tax related expenditures. Take this to an accountant and your work is done.

8

THE COMPOSER'S PLACE IN THE BUSINESS OF MUSIC

Many people are involved in bringing a choral piece to realization. The team includes the composer, publisher, editor, engraver/computer person, printer, retailer, conductor, choir, and the audience. Subsidiary members of the team include ticket sellers, stage personnel, and advertising agents. Sometimes the team includes a person who pays the composer to create—the commissioner of the piece. Choral music is a big business. Composers don't just interact with publishers. They assume different roles as they deal with the various members of the choral music business team.

The composer and the commissioning person

Some composers only write music on a commission basis. This is usually not by choice, but because they are so in demand they have no time for other creative endeavors. When a composer arrives at this level, he/she is truly in the business of composing.

Occasionally a composer can generate a

commission opportunity by presenting an idea for a piece to a conductor. The conductor might be a personal friend, or someone with whom the composer has worked. If the composer is not well-known, the fee for this commission may by minimal. The goal here is not monetary; it is for the composer to begin to get established as one who does commissions, and to provide an opportunity for him or her to learn from the experience of working with a conductor.

Some conductors regularly commission music. Others do so for special occasions. School anniversaries— twenty-five, fifty, one hundred year—are frequently commemorated with commissioned works. Pieces are commissioned on the death of someone close to the choir, on the retirement of a conductor, for a choir to take on tour, to honor a specific ethnic group. Many community choirs, semi-professional choirs, and pop groups make a habit of commissioning works for the interest and prestige it adds to their programs.

A composer writing a commissioned piece is subject to the wishes of the person for whom he/she is now working. No matter the conditions, it is important that the composer retain artistic control. And, the composer should consider what type of piece will have a chance at being published—one with a universally appealing text, one whose performance needs can be met by many choirs. Sometimes the composer must do some negotiating to convince the commissioning person to compromise his/her demands. If publication of the piece does not seem a possibility, the price for the commission should be commensurately higher. Many extended works will fall into this category.

The commissioning person may be as anxious for the piece to be published as is the composer. If this is the case, the composer must be careful not to offer any promises which cannot be kept.

The composer as PR agent

Some composers are adept at networking and like to advance the cause of their own music. Publishers will be happy to provide complimentary copies of a piece when a composer indicates these copies will be used to promote the piece. Some composers maintain databases of people who like their music and regularly apprise these people of their new publications. Others carry newly published pieces with them when they attend meetings and share them with friends. Some present choral workshops and feature their own music. There is no shame in being proud of your own creations and wanting to share them. Publishers appreciate composers who can help promote their own music.

The composer as conductor

What could be more exciting than conducting your own composition! If you have fine conducting skills, you may be asked to do just that. If your conducting skills are inadequate and you are asked, be gracious and refuse the invitation. There is that famous Shaker song, "Tis the gift to be simple... to come down where you ought to be." If that place is enjoying your piece as a member of the audience, it is best you be there.

The composer
as critical advisor to a director

If you are asked to help with the rehearsal preparation of a new piece of your creation, do so. Many conductors love to work with composers this way.

If you hear things going wrong in a rehearsal and you have not been asked to help, it is best to leave the conductor alone to do his/her job. The exception: you see the problem stems from a lack of directive in the score. In this case, you can legitimately offer help while accepting "blame" for the omission. If the director is insecure, your presence alone may add to that insecurity; your stepping in to "help" might just make matters worse. Sensitivity to the situation is a must. In the business world of music, it is important to know your place at all times.

The composer as a member
of a performing rights organization

Some composers (and publishers) affiliate with a performing rights organization to generate more income from their music. These organizations license the public performance of music. They collect fees for titles that are the creation of their members. They subsequently pay a portion of the fees to those composers and publishers.

There are three such organizations in the United States: ASCAP, the American Society of Composers, Authors and Publishers; BMI, Broadcast Music, Incorporated; and SESAC, formerly called the Society of European Stage Authors and Composers, now active in the United States and simply called SESAC.

A composer can become a member in one of these organizations upon publication of one title. It is not possible to join more than one organization. The membership fee and dues for all three are minimal. Composers interested in learning more about these organizations may contact them directly. (Addresses are in the appendix.) Since the organizations are in competition for members, they should welcome your inquiry. If possible, personally visit their headquarters.

As mentioned earlier, these organizations can assist in the search for the copyright owner of a piece. They keep up-to-date records of all of their member publishers. In the popular music business, one publisher may assume several names. Or a copyright may transfer several times to different publishers. When looking for the copyright owner of such a piece, these organizations become an invaluable resource.

The composer as publisher

Being a publisher is a lot of work. It requires great commitment, much money invested, and an immense amount of time. Composers sometimes try to publish their own compositions. This is not easy to do. Marketing ten pieces can take as much effort as marketing two hundred. The monetary returns on ten compositions will be too small to merit the time and effort needed to properly present them.

Some composers establish a publishing company, yet only publish their own pieces. This deceives no one. This composer will be promoting his/her own music with no validation from an outside source—a very difficult thing to do. Because it is awkward to represent oneself, actors and writers have agents. Composers have publishers. If you are truly a talented composer, your time is best spent composing. Let a publisher worry about all the other problems.

The composer as an advocate for integrity

The entire choral music business exists solely because of the creations of composers. A composer must join with the publisher and the retailer in being an advocate for the education of all musicians to one fact: it is illegal to photocopy music.

Earlier it was suggested that composers judiciously photocopy their unpublished music. When giving unpublished music to a choir, give them the number of copies they need, all clearly marked with a copyright notice. For commissioned works, most composers prepare computer scores and have them bound. The composer includes the cost of this preparation in the commission fee. As owner of the copyright, do not allow choral directors to make additional copies. When they are done with the music, it may be wise to request they return it to you. If you plan on getting the piece published, you do not want pre-publication copies circulating. Upon publication, show your appreciation to the director by presenting him/her with published copies. Your publisher should be willing to provide these copies to you at cost, or at a large discount, or free depending on the circumstances.

Do what you can to help educate choral musicians. This education can include your sharing a booklet titled *The United States Copyright Law*. It was jointly prepared by the Music Publishers' Association of the United States, the Music Educators National Conference, the Music Teachers National Association, the National Association of Schools of Music, and the National Music Publishers' Association. The booklet is available from the Music Publishers' Association. (Address in appendix) Pages from it may be photocopied.

An informative, imposing poster titled *Integrity and Our Art* was produced by the Music Publishers' Association of the United States, the Church Music Publishers' Association, and the Retail Print Music Dealers Association. This poster is reproduced in the appendix of this book. It too may be photocopied.

The composer as composer

Those called to the art of composing carry a unique responsibility: composers create the product that shapes the choral art. This tremendous challenge is not to be borne lightly. Hopefully, the ideas put forth in this book will stimulate growth, and provide greater understanding of ways to meet this challenge.

The challenge: Checklist for the composer

- Compose as a knowledgeable singer
- Compose as an experienced choir singer
- Compose as one who has studied the art and craft of music composition

APPENDIX

82

APPENDIX

Reference, page three and four

1. Igor Stravinsky, *Poetics of Music,*
   Cambridge, Massachusetts: Harvard University Press, 1942, p.65
2. ibid., page 76

Recommended books

Choral Music, A Norton Historical Anthology
   ed. Ray Robinson,
   W.W. Norton and Co., NY, 1978
   Complete scores of a representative group of famous choral
   compositions starting with chants from the year 1300.

Contemporary Choral Arranging
   Arthur E. Ostrander and Dana Wilson
   Prentice Hall, Englewood Cliffs, NJ, 1986
   Recommended by teachers of choral arranging.

Music in Print
   Musicdata, Inc.
   PO Box, 48010, Philadelphia, PA, 19144-8010
   Annual listings of titles, composers, and their publishers.
   Musicdata also publishes volumes for both sacred and secular
   music.

Music Notation, A Manual of Modern Practice
   Gardner Reed, Taplinger Publishing Co., New York, NY, 1979
   A valuable reference for the composer; limited only by its
   publication date–no discussion of computer notation.

Standard Music Notation Practice, pamphlet
   Music Publishers' Association of the United States
   A free pamphlet available from the above organization.
   (address listed in appendix under composer contacts)

This Business of Music
> Sidney Shemel and M. William Krasilovsky
> Billboard Publications, N.Y., 1985
> A practical guide to the music industry for publishers, writers,
> record companies, producers, artists, and agents.

The Technique of Choral Composition
> Archibald T. Davison
> Harvard University Press, 1966.
> A useful reference for the choral composer.
> Out of print; available in many college libraries.

The United States Copyright Law, pamphlet
> Music Publishers' Association of the United States,
> the Music Educators National Conference,
> the Music Teachers National Association,
> the National Association of Schools of Music,
> and the National Music Publishers' Association.
> A free pamphlet jointly published by the above organizations;
> presents the copyright law in easily understood language.
> Available from the Music Publisher's Association of the U.S.
> (address listed in appendix under composer contacts)

You, the Singer
> Barbara Harlow
> Hinshaw Music, Inc., 1985
> A textbook for voice study that includes discussions of the
> treatment of words in songs, and the characteristics of vowels
> and consonants.

COMPOSER CONTACTS

PERFORMING RIGHTS ORGANIZATIONS

ASCAP
1 Lincoln Plaza
New York, NY 10023
(212) 621–6000

7920 Sunset Boulevard
Los Angeles, CA 90046
(213) 883–1000

2 Music Square West
Nashville, TN 37203
(615) 742–5000

Kingsbury Center
350 West Hubbard Street
Chicago, IL 60610
(312) 527–9775

52 Haymarket
London SW1 Y4RP England
(011–44–71) 973–0069

First National Bank Building
1519 Ponce De Leon Avenue
Santurce, Puerto Rico 00910
(809) 725–1688

BMI
320 West 57th Street
New York, NY 10019
(212) 586–2000

8730 Sunset Boulevard
Third Floor West
Los Angeles, CA 90069
(213) 659–9109

10 Music Square East
Nashville, TN 37203
(615) 259–3625

79 Harley House
Marylebone Road
London, NY1 5HN England
(011–44–71) 935–8517

SESAC
156 West 56th Street
New York, NY 10019
(212) 556–3450

55 Music Square East
Nashville, TN 37203
(615) 320–0055

COPYRIGHT REGISTRATION

Register of Copyrights
Library of Congress
Washington DC, 20559

*Contact for registration of copyright and current copyright
information regarding forms and fees*

PUBLISHER ORGANIZATIONS

Music Publishers' Association of the U.S.
711 Third Ave.
New York, NY 10017

Contact for Copyright Brochure
Contact for list of publisher members
Contact for Standard Music Notation Practice booklet

National Music Publishers' Association
205 East 42nd Street
New York, NY 10017

Membership comprised of publishers of pop music

Retail Print Music Dealers Association
4020 McEwen, Suite 105
Dallas, TX 75244
(212) 233–9107

*Membership comprised of retail music dealers; publishers join as
associate members.*

CONSERVATIVE VOCAL RANGES

CHILDREN'S CHORUS

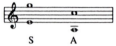

These ranges apply to most eight–twelve year old singers. Children should be encouraged to develop their head voices, those notes on, not below the treble staff. With proper training, child sopranos are capable of singing high B's with ease. Unison writing in the soprano range works well for girls this age–the girl's alto voice does not begin to develop until the teen years. Some boy's voices will have begun to change–they can sing alto with ease. Children should not be allowed to force their voices to gain volume–bad vocal habits and damage to the voice may be the result.

JUNIOR HIGH SCHOOL CHORUS

Junior high basses age thirteen have been known to sing low F's, however, this is most unusual. The tenor range given here accommodates the changing voice. Boys stay in this limited range for varied amounts of time. Some are never limited to this range, going directly to bass when their voices change. The alto voice is just beginning to develop; young girls should be encouraged to alternate between singing soprano and alto. As with children, the junior high voice is light in timbre. This age group should not be asked to force their voices to sing with a loud, mature tone. Bad vocal habits will be the result, and perhaps damage to the voice.

HIGH SCHOOL CHORUS

S   A   T   B

High school choirs will have some singers that can sing beyond these ranges. Many tenors of all ages cannot go below the E and make an audible sound. As the tenor voice is just developing in high school, it is wise not to force these singers to any extremes. High school seniors often pride themselves on singing lower than the G given here. Ethnic differences combine with early maturity and play a part in extending these ranges. One all–black high school choir had four mature seventeen year old boys who could sing low D's. A Hispanic high school choir was endowed with several tenors that sang high A's with ease. The conservative range remains the safest to use if music is targeted for this age group.

ADULT CHORUS

S   A   T   B

This conservative range will apply to all ages but seniors. Seniors lose the high notes of their range. All top notes should be a third lower for them.

The professional adult choir will have basses capable of singing low E's and sopranos capable of high B's. Altos often are expected to sing a low F, or an E a note high than the range given here. Tenors may be expected to sing a high A.

INTEGRITY AND OUR ART

It's a matter of dollars and sense...
Imagine yourself as a *publisher* of *printed sheet music...*
A *composer* comes to you with a *wonderful new composition...*
You decide to *publish* the *new piece.*

You *pay* the composer, you *pay* your editor,
you *pay* your engraver, you *pay* your printer,
and *pay* your promotional costs, you *pay* all your copyright
and legal fees, you *pay* your overhead, and you get the *piece*
into *print.*

You send it to stores around the country.
They *pay* you for the music,
they promote it and they *sell* some of the new piece.

Some of the customers who *buy* it make *illegal copies* of it...
"Just for church," "For educational purposes,"
"For a non-profit organization," "Just for the words," etc.

The remaining published copies of the new piece
are sold in decreasing amounts.
Since customers are copying it,
not as many get sold as had been expected.
The stores hardly order any more from you, the publisher.

You look at the *money* you *spent* to *publish* the piece.
It *greatly exceeds* the *money* you are *making*
from the sale of the piece.
You have to make a *business* decision.

How to Get Your Choral Composition Published

You must stay in business so that you can keep
providing music for the world
and *present new music* to the world, so...
You *raise the price* when you reprint a small batch to satisfy
the meager orders.

The *customers* grumble about the increased price
and *keep on copying,* and the vicious cycle continues.

Finally, because of the low demand, and the cost involved,
you cannot justify keeping the piece published,
and you have to put it *permanently out of print.*

And another wonderful piece of music,
the creative offering of a fellow musician,
is lost to the world.

Now, imagine yourself as a *composer...*

Copying music is not only illegal,
it is immoral and unconscionable.
Do something about it. Don't copy music yourself.
Convince your fellow musicians not to copy music.
It's the only thing that makes any sense.

From a poster jointly prepared by: the Music Publishers' Association
of the United States, the Church Music Publishers' Association, and the
Retail Print Music Dealers Association.

About the Author

Barbara Harlow has pursued a lifelong interest in music, and publishing/writing/editing. She served as editor of four school papers and yearbooks commencing with grade six, and this same year was awarded the first of many scholarships and awards for her musical ability. She has had several choral compositions published, and is the author of a voice textbook, *You, the Singer,* published by Hinshaw Music. A graduate of the University of Southern California, with a Masters Degree in choral composition from California State University at Fullerton, she has had thirty years of choral teaching experience working at all levels, elementary through college. In addition to her primary assignment as choral director, she has taught music theory, piano, voice and guitar. She is an accomplished accompanist, and for several years sang with the Roger Wagner Chorale in Los Angeles. Barbara is president/owner of Santa Barbara Music Publishing, a company "dedicated to nurturing the choral art."